If lost, please return to:

D1744523

PRODUCTIVE CHRISTIAN JOURNAL

A 12 week guide to accomplish your goals and grow your faith.

by Brandon Hilgemann

Contents

How to Do This

This journal changed my life. In 2015, I was working full-time as a pastor and pulling late nights to get a masters degree in theology. My wife was also working night shifts as a nurse, and we had two little kids at home. So she had the kids in the morning, I had them after work, and we saw each other somewhere in between. Worse still, I was unhealthy and miserable because I was so busy doing everything else that I wasn't taking care of myself. My life was out of control. I was spiritually, physically, mentally, and emotionally drained. I needed a better way to stay focused on the most important things and get more done.

So in 2016, I began playing around with this productivity journaling system, making small tweaks as I went along. Using this system over the next few years, I started waking up early, studying the Bible more, exercising daily, spending more time with my family, and accomplishing big goals with the little time I had. I graduated with honors, wrote two books, and unexpectedly stepped into God's call to be a writer. The journal didn't do the work for me, but it sure helped.

I created this journal for myself. But if you need help getting more done, staying focused on your goals, and starting a daily routine to change your life, it'll help you too.

Here's how it works. Look over the following sample pages (p.2-4), and then I'll explain:

MONDAY *(Sample)*

11/26/18

Morning Reps

● Read *(Bible Study)*   ● Exercise   ● Pray

- -

Big Goal

In _90_ days, I will _write the first draft of a book._

Next Step: _Write book outline_

- -

Top Tasks

	Est. Time
● Brainstorm all the topics the book needs to cover	2 hr
○ Organize each topic under chapter headings	1 hr
○ Arrange chapters to create outline first draft	30 min

If Time

○ List research materials for book	1 hr
○ Respond to email	20 min
○ Schedule social media posts	30 min
○ Order research materials	15 min
○ Pick up groceries	30 min
○ Write 500 words	1 hr
○ Organize desk	1 hr
○ Take out trash	5 min
○ Text Joe, Matt, Chris, Sarah, and Dennis	10 min

- -

Evening Prep

○ Plan   ○ Read   ○ Pray

Read

Romans 16

Explain

Paul has not yet been to Rome, but he still knows so many people there. He says he has worked with many of them. So he doesn't just know them from a distance. These are probably believers he has met in his missionary travels who now live in Rome. The great number shows how many people Paul has influenced and also how large the church in Rome has grown. Paul must have been highly relational and have had a great memory of people's names.

Apply

I need to emphasize my relationship with people more. I can tend to be a hermit most of the week. People have infinite value, and I don't put enough time into relationships to show them how much I value them. So today I will text some of the people I haven't talked to in a long time, and I will add it to my task list so I don't forget!

Pray

Father, thank you for your great love for all people, even a sinner like me. Forgive me for not being more people-oriented. Help me to be more relational like Paul and grow to love people like you do.

WEEKEND REVIEW *(Sample)*

Biggest win

I finished the outline for my book.

- -

Greatest problem
I realized that there are still a lot of things I need to research before I start writing.

- -

Possible solutions to the problem:

I will list all of topics I need to research, and focus extra time each day and in the evenings doing reading and taking detailed notes.

- -

Relationship Goals

Who	What	When
● Taryn (wife)	Plan date night	Friday
○ Ashlyn (daughter)	Practice volleyball	Thursday
○ Jaxon (son)	Play video games	Saturday
○ Amy	Send "Thank You" card	Monday
○ Justin	Grab coffee	Wednesday
○ Mom	Call	Sunday
○		

Goal

In __84__ days, I will *write the first draft of a book.*

- -

This Week's Next Step:

Write book outline.

Accomplished?

 Yes ◯ No

- -

Next Week's Next Step:

Compile research notes for chapters 1-3.

- -

Goal Progress

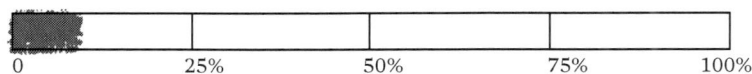

0	25%	50%	75%	100%

25% = *Outline and research complete.*

50% = *Chapter 1-3 written*

75% = *Chapter 4-6 written*

100% = Goal Achieved!

WEEKDAYS (p.2-3)

Every weekday, the journal walks you through the five essential elements of a highly productive day: (1) Morning Reps, (2) Big Goal, (3) Top Tasks, (4) Evening Prep, and (5) Bible Study.

1. Morning Reps

How you begin the day will set the tone for the rest of your day. Your Morning Reps are the daily habits you need that often get dropped because they're not urgent. If you don't make time for these habits, you won't find time for them.

For me, REPs is an acronym for my routine: Read, Exercise, Pray. When I begin the day with my REPs, I've filled my tank so I'm not running on empty all day.

How will you start your days? You can use my routine or find whatever you need for a great start. Maybe you simply need a shower, a cup of coffee, and a place to sit and be still for a minute. Find what works for you and make time for it.

2. Big Goal

Drift happens. Life is so busy that we naturally drift from our priorities if we aren't careful. How many times have we spent the day putting out fires only to wonder, what did we even get done? We checked things off the to-do list but didn't get closer to our goal.

The Big Goal section is designed to help keep you from drifting. A goal is just a dream with a deadline. So every day, you'll write down your goal, and count down the days left until you want to accomplish it. And since it often takes many small steps to reach a big goal, you'll also write your next step toward the goal.

What's your big goal? Be specific. It could be to increase sales by 10%, launch a new ministry, or lose ten pounds. Whatever it is, the best way to accomplish a big goal is to write it down, keep it in front of you, and focus on the next small step.

3. Top Tasks

This journal is more than a to-do list. I want you to get in the habit of asking yourself every day, "What are the three most important things I need to do today?" These are the three things that, if you do nothing else, it's still a productive day. There's also space to list other important tasks that you need to do if you have time.

For each task, there's an area for you to estimate the amount of time it'll take to do. This can help you can manage your time better. For example, if you find that you have fifteen minutes between meetings, it wouldn't make sense to start a task that'll take an hour, but there may be something on your list that only takes ten minutes that you could do.

Writing your top tasks its a simple habit that'll keep you focused on the things that make the greatest impact with your limited time.

4. Evening Prep

Just as you need to start the day off with good habits, you also need to end your day with habits that'll set you up to win tomorrow. The Evening Prep section is a space to list your evening routine. For me, once again, PReP is an acrostic for Plan, Read, Pray. I plan the next day in my journal, read a book, and end the day with prayer.

You can use my Plan, Read, Pray system or pick whatever you need to do every night to prepare for the next day. It could be something like laying out clothes, packing lunch, or working out. Start a habit of doing those things every night to prepare yourself to win the next day.

5. Bible Study

Christians are people of the Bible. So it would be hard to say we've had a productive week if we've neglected to spend time in God's Word. This journal is designed to help you make Bible Study a habit. I suggest doing it in either your morning or evening routine. The format is simple. Reap is, you've guessed it, another acrostic. REAP stands for Read, Explain, Apply, Pray. Plus, it's a reminder of why we study the Bible: We want to reap the fruit of planting God's word in our hearts (Psalm 1).

Read: Read a section of the Bible. You could do one chapter a day through a book of the Bible, or you could follow any reading plan using multiple chapters. If it's a long section, pull out a key verse or two that you want to focus on.

Explain: Explain what you read. Here's where this method differs from others. Most systems say to *examine* the verse, but *explaining* is better. (1) It's not enough to study the Bible; you also have to interpret what it says. (2) The best way to learn something is to explain it to someone else. And (3) nothing drives you to study the Bible deeper than trying to explain it and realizing you can't.

Apply: How will you apply this to your life? Make it as action-oriented as possible (James 1:22). For example, in the sample page, I read Romans 16 and saw the long list of Paul's friends that he greets. It convicted me that I haven't reached out to some people in a while. So I applied the verse by texting them. Texting was better than just writing, "I need to foster better relationships." Apply it to your task list if you can.

Pray: Pray about it. Prayer is simply talking to God. So I'll jot a few bullet points in this section about things I need to pray about. Then, I'll pause to pray and talk to God about what I read. You could also write out your prayer if you want (like I did in the sample page).

WEEKEND REVIEW (p.4-5)

At the end of every week, there's a weekend review section that's fairly self-explanatory.

1. Win, Problem, and Solution

The first three sections walk you through a simple review of your week. First, you'll identify your biggest win so you can celebrate what you've accomplished. Second, you'll identify the greatest problem you're facing at the moment. Third, you'll think of a potential solution to the problem. By identifying a win and coming up with a potential solution to your biggest problem, you end the week on a positive note, building momentum going into the next week.

2. Relationship Goals

The relationship goals section is designed to help you be more intentional with your relationships, so you don't spend all your time with projects instead of people. We often plan our work but rarely plan our relationships. Here you can list some of your important relationships and plan what you want to do for them. How will you serve, surprise, or spend time with these people this week?

3. Goal and Next Steps

On the second page of the Weekend Review, you remind yourself again of your goal, continuing to count down the days until you plan to reach it. Then, you review your next step for the week. If you accomplished it, plan your next step for the upcoming week. If you did not accomplish your next step, write it again for next week's next step. By planning your next step over the weekend, you can begin the next week running, already knowing where you're going.

4. Goal Progress

Accomplishing a big goal can be frustrating because it's hard to see incremental progress. The goal progress bar is a simple way to visualize the progress you've made towards your goal. Start by identifying a few mile markers along the way to your goal. Then, estimate the progress you've made. If you've made it 25%, 50%, and 75% to your goal, what will that look like? Hitting these milestones as you fill that progress bar more every week will keep you encouraged and feeling the progress. It's become one of my favorite parts of the week.

Are You Ready?

Set your first goal and begin. You can do this! It won't be easy at first, and you may need to adjust some things here and there to find what works for you, but I promise you that it will be worth it. You won't believe how your life can change when you follow God and make the best use of the time he has entrusted to you.

"Look carefully then how you walk, not as unwise but as wise, making the best use of the time, because the days are evil."

Ephesians 5:15-16 ESV

Week 1

MONDAY

Morning Reps

○ ○ ○

Big Goal

In ___ days, I will _____

Next Step: _____

Top Tasks   Est. Time

○ |

○ |

○ |

If Time

○ |

○ |

○ |

○ |

○ |

○ |

○ |

○ |

○ |

Evening Prep

○ ○ ○

Read

Explain

Apply

Pray

TUESDAY   / /

Morning Reps

○   ○   ○

- -

Big Goal

In ____ days, I will _____

Next Step: _____

- -

Top Tasks   Est. Time

○ _____ |

○ _____ |

○ _____ |

If Time

○ _____ |

○ _____ |

○ _____ |

○ _____ |

○ _____ |

○ _____ |

○ _____ |

○ _____ |

○ _____ |

- -

Evening Prep

○   ○   ○

Read

Explain

Apply

Pray

/ /

Morning Reps

○   ○   ○

- -

Big Goal

In ___ days, I will _____

Next Step: _____

- -

Top Tasks   Est. Time

○

○

○

If Time

○

○

○

○

○

○

○

○

○

- -

Evening Prep

○   ○   ○

16

Read

- -

Explain

- -

Apply

- -

Pray

THURSDAY   / /

Morning Reps

○   ○   ○

- -

Big Goal

In ___ days, I will _____

Next Step: _____

- -

Top Tasks   Est. Time

○

○

○

If Time

○

○

○

○

○

○

○

○

○

- -

Evening Prep

○   ○   ○

18

Read

Explain

Apply

Pray

FRIDAY

Morning Reps

○   ○   ○

Big Goal

In ___ days, I will _____

Next Step: _____

Top Tasks   Est. Time

○

○

○

If Time

○

○

○

○

○

○

○

○

○

Evening Prep

○   ○   ○

Read

Explain

Apply

Pray

WEEKEND REVIEW

Biggest win

- -

Greatest problem

- -

Possible solutions to the problem:

- -

Relationship Goals

Who	What	When
○		
○		
○		
○		
○		
○		
○		

Goal

In _____ days, I will _____

- -

This Week's Next Step:

Accomplished?

○ Yes ○ No

- -

Next Week's Next Step:

- -

Goal Progress

0	25%	50%	75%	100%

25% =

50% =

75% =

100% = Goal Achieved!

"Whatever you do, work heartily, as for the Lord and not for men."

Colossians 3:23 ESV

Week 2

MONDAY

/ /

Morning Reps

◯ ◯ ◯

Big Goal

In ___ days, I will _____

Next Step: _____

Top Tasks

Est. Time

◯

◯

◯

If Time

◯

◯

◯

◯

◯

◯

◯

◯

◯

Evening Prep

◯ ◯ ◯

Read

Explain

Apply

Pray

TUESDAY

/ /

Morning Reps

○   ○   ○

- -

Big Goal

In ____ days, I will _____

Next Step: _____

- -

Top Tasks   Est. Time

○ ....

○ ....

○ ....

If Time

○ ....

○ ....

○ ....

○ ....

○ ....

○ ....

○ ....

○ ....

○ ....

- -

Evening Prep

○   ○   ○

Read

Explain

Apply

Pray

WEDNESDAY   /   /

Morning Reps
○   ○   ○

- -

Big Goal
In ___ days, I will _____

Next Step: _____

- -

Top Tasks   Est. Time
○

○

○

If Time
○

○

○

○

○

○

○

○

○

- -

Evening Prep
○   ○   ○

Read

Explain

Apply

Pray

THURSDAY

/ /

Morning Reps

○　　　　　　　　　○　　　　　　　　　○

- -

Big Goal

In ＿＿ days, I will ＿＿＿＿＿＿＿＿＿＿＿＿＿＿＿＿＿＿＿＿＿＿

Next Step: ＿＿＿＿＿＿＿＿＿＿＿＿＿＿＿＿＿＿＿＿＿＿＿＿

- -

Top Tasks   **Est. Time**

○

○

○

If Time

○

○

○

○

○

○

○

○

○

- -

Evening Prep

○　　　　　　　　　○　　　　　　　　　○

32

Read

Explain

Apply

Pray

FRIDAY

/ /

Morning Reps

○   ○   ○

- -

Big Goal

In _____ days, I will _____

Next Step: _____

- -

Top Tasks   Est. Time

○

○

○

If Time

○

○

○

○

○

○

○

○

○

- -

Evening Prep

○   ○   ○

Read

Explain

Apply

Pray

WEEKEND REVIEW

Biggest win

- -

Greatest problem

- -

Possible solutions to the problem:

- -

Relationship Goals

Who	What	When
○		
○		
○		
○		
○		
○		
○		

Goal

In ____ days, I will _____

- -

This Week's Next Step:

Accomplished?

○ Yes ○ No

- -

Next Week's Next Step:

- -

Goal Progress

0	25%	50%	75%	100%

25% =

50% =

75% =

100% = Goal Achieved!

"Our days may come to seventy years, or eighty, if our strength endures; yet the best of them are but trouble and sorrow, for they quickly pass, and we fly away.... Teach us to number our days, that we may gain a heart of wisdom."

Psalm 90:10, 12 NIV

Week 3

MONDAY

/ /

Morning Reps

○ ○ ○

Big Goal

In ___ days, I will _____

Next Step: _____

Top Tasks Est. Time

○

○

○

If Time

○

○

○

○

○

○

○

○

○

Evening Prep

○ ○ ○

Read

- -

Explain

.

- -

Apply

- -

Pray

TUESDAY

/ /

Morning Reps

○   ○   ○

- -

Big Goal

In ___ days, I will _____

Next Step: _____

- -

Top Tasks   Est. Time

○

○

○

If Time

○

○

○

○

○

○

○

○

○

- -

Evening Prep

○   ○   ○

Read

Explain

Apply

Pray

WEDNESDAY

Morning Reps

○ ○ ○

- -

Big Goal

In ___ days, I will _____

Next Step: _____

- -

Top Tasks   **Est. Time**

○

○

○

If Time

○

○

○

○

○

○

○

○

○

Evening Prep

○ ○ ○

Read

Explain

Apply

Pray

THURSDAY

Morning Reps

○   ○   ○

- -

Big Goal

In ___ days, I will _____

Next Step: _____

- -

Top Tasks   **Est. Time**

○

○

○

If Time

○

○

○

○

○

○

○

○

○

- -

Evening Prep

○   ○   ○

Read

Explain

Apply

Pray

FRIDAY

/   /

Morning Reps

○   ○   ○

- -

Big Goal

In ___ days, I will _____

Next Step: _____

- -

Top Tasks   Est. Time

○

○

○

If Time

○

○

○

○

○

○

○

○

○

- -

Evening Prep

○   ○   ○

Read

Explain

Apply

Pray

WEEKEND REVIEW

Biggest win

Greatest problem

Possible solutions to the problem:

Relationship Goals

Who	What	When
○		
○		
○		
○		
○		
○		
○		

Goal

In ____ days, I will _____

- -

This Week's Next Step:

Accomplished?

○ Yes ○ No

- -

Next Week's Next Step:

- -

Goal Progress

0	25%	50%	75%	100%

25% =

50% =

75% =

100% = Goal Achieved!

"Let us not become weary in doing good, for at the proper time we will reap a harvest if we do not give up."

Galatians 6:9 NIV

Week 4

MONDAY

/ /

Morning Reps

○   ○   ○

- -

Big Goal

In ___ days, I will _____

Next Step: _____

- -

Top Tasks   Est. Time

○ _____

○ _____

○ _____

If Time

○ _____

○ _____

○ _____

○ _____

○ _____

○ _____

○ _____

○ _____

○ _____

- -

Evening Prep

○   ○   ○

Read

Explain

Apply

Pray

TUESDAY

/ /

Morning Reps

○   ○   ○

- -

Big Goal

In ___ days, I will _____

Next Step: _____

- -

Top Tasks   Est. Time

○

○ |

○ |

If Time

○ |

○ |

○ |

○ |

○ |

○ |

○ |

○ |

○ |

- -

Evening Prep

○   ○   ○

Read

Explain

Apply

Pray

WEDNESDAY

/ /

Morning Reps

○　　　　　　　　○　　　　　　　　○

- -

Big Goal

In ___ days, I will _____

Next Step: _____

- -

Top Tasks　　　　　　　　　　　　　　　　　　　　　Est. Time

○

○

○

If Time

○

○

○

○

○

○

○

○

○

- -

Evening Prep

○　　　　　　　　○　　　　　　　　○

Read

Explain

Apply

Pray

THURSDAY

Morning Reps

○   ○   ○

- -

Big Goal

In ____ days, I will _____

Next Step: _____

- -

Top Tasks   Est. Time

○

○

○

If Time

○

○

○

○

○

○

○

○

○

- -

Evening Prep

○   ○   ○

Read

Explain

Apply

Pray

FRIDAY

/ /

Morning Reps

○   ○   ○

- -

Big Goal

In ___ days, I will _____

Next Step: _____

- -

Top Tasks   Est. Time

○ ....

○ ....

○ ....

If Time

○ ....

○ ....

○ ....

○ ....

○ ....

○ ....

○ ....

○ ....

○ ....

- -

Evening Prep

○   ○   ○

Read

Explain

Apply

Pray

WEEKEND REVIEW

Biggest win

Greatest problem

Possible solutions to the problem:

Relationship Goals

Who	What	When
○		
○		
○		
○		
○		
○		
○		

Goal

In ____ days, I will _____

- -

This Week's Next Step:

Accomplished?

○ Yes ○ No

- -

Next Week's Next Step:

- -

Goal Progress

0	25%	50%	75%	100%

25% =

50% =

75% =

100% = Goal Achieved!

"There is profit in all hard work, but endless talk leads only to poverty."

Proverbs 14:23 CSB

Week 5

MONDAY

Morning Reps

○ ○ ○

Big Goal

In ___ days, I will _____

Next Step: _____

Top Tasks   Est. Time

○

○

○

If Time

○

○

○

○

○

○

○

○

○

Evening Prep

○ ○ ○

68

Read

- -

Explain

- -

Apply

- -

Pray

TUESDAY   / /

Morning Reps

○   ○   ○

- -

Big Goal

In ___ days, I will _____

Next Step: _____

- -

Top Tasks   **Est. Time**

○

○

○

If Time

○

○

○

○

○

○

○

○

○

- -

Evening Prep

○   ○   ○

Read

Explain

Apply

Pray

／　／

Morning Reps

○　　　　　　　　　○　　　　　　　　　○

- -

Big Goal

In ____ days, I will _____

Next Step: _____

- -

Top Tasks   Est. Time

○ _____

○ _____

○ _____

If Time

○ _____

○ _____

○ _____

○ _____

○ _____

○ _____

○ _____

○ _____

○ _____

- -

Evening Prep

○　　　　　　　　　○　　　　　　　　　○

Read

- -

Explain

- -

Apply

- -

Pray

THURSDAY

/ /

Morning Reps

○　　　　　　　　○　　　　　　　　○

- -

Big Goal

In ___ days, I will _____

Next Step: _____

- -

Top Tasks   Est. Time

○

○

○

If Time

○

○

○

○

○

○

○

○

○

- -

Evening Prep

○　　　　　　　　○　　　　　　　　○

Read

Explain

Apply

Pray

FRIDAY

/ /

Morning Reps

○ ○ ○

- -

Big Goal

In ____ days, I will _____

Next Step: _____

- -

Top Tasks	Est. Time
○	
○	
○	

If Time

○	
○	
○	
○	
○	
○	
○	
○	
○	

- -

Evening Prep

○ ○ ○

Read

Explain

Apply

Pray

WEEKEND REVIEW

Biggest win

Greatest problem

Possible solutions to the problem:

Relationship Goals

Who	What	When
○		
○		
○		
○		
○		
○		
○		

Goal

In ____ days, I will _____

This Week's Next Step:

Accomplished?

○ Yes ○ No

Next Week's Next Step:

Goal Progress

0	25%	50%	75%	100%

25% =

50% =

75% =

100% = Goal Achieved!

"And whatever you do, in word or deed, do everything in the name of the Lord Jesus, giving thanks to God the Father through him."

Colossians 3:17 ESV

Week 6

MONDAY

/ /

Morning Reps

○   ○   ○

- -

Big Goal

In ___ days, I will _____

Next Step: _____

- -

Top Tasks   Est. Time

○

○

○

If Time

○

○

○

○

○

○

○

○

○

- -

Evening Prep

○   ○   ○

Read

Explain

Apply

Pray

TUESDAY   / /

Morning Reps

○   ○   ○

- -

Big Goal

In ____ days, I will _____

Next Step: _____

- -

Top Tasks   Est. Time

○

○

○

If Time

○

○

○

○

○

○

○

○

○

- -

Evening Prep

○   ○   ○

84

Read

Explain

Apply

Pray

WEDNESDAY   /   /

Morning Reps

○   ○   ○

- -

Big Goal

In ___ days, I will _____

Next Step: _____

- -

Top Tasks   Est. Time

○

○

○

If Time

○

○

○

○

○

○

○

○

○

- -

Evening Prep

○   ○   ○

Read

Explain

Apply

Pray

THURSDAY   / /

Morning Reps
○   ○   ○

- -

Big Goal
In ___ days, I will _____

Next Step: _____

- -

Top Tasks   Est. Time
○
....
○
....
○
....

If Time
○
....
○
....
○
....
○
....
○
....
○
....
○
....
○
....
○
- -

Evening Prep
○   ○   ○

Read

Explain

Apply

Pray

FRIDAY

/ /

Morning Reps

○   ○   ○

- -

Big Goal

In ___ days, I will _____

Next Step: _____

- -

Top Tasks   Est. Time

○

○

○

If Time

○

○

○

○

○

○

○

○

○

Evening Prep

○   ○   ○

Read

Explain

Apply

Pray

WEEKEND REVIEW

Biggest win

- -

Greatest problem

- -

Possible solutions to the problem:

- -

Relationship Goals

Who	What	When
○		
○		
○		
○		
○		
○		
○		

Goal

In _____ days, I will _____

- -

This Week's Next Step:

Accomplished?

○ Yes   ○ No

- -

Next Week's Next Step:

- -

Goal Progress

0	25%	50%	75%	100%

25% =

50% =

75% =

100% = Goal Achieved!

"Go to the ant, O sluggard; consider her ways, and be wise. Without having any chief, officer, or ruler, she prepares her bread in summer and gathers her food in harvest. How long will you lie there, O sluggard? When will you arise from your sleep? A little sleep, a little slumber, a little folding of the hands to rest, and poverty will come upon you like a robber, and want like an armed man."

Proverbs 6:6-11 ESV

Week 7

MONDAY

Morning Reps

○   ○   ○

- -

Big Goal

In ___ days, I will _____

Next Step: _____

- -

Top Tasks   **Est. Time**

○

○

○

If Time

○

○

○

○

○

○

○

○

○

- -

Evening Prep

○   ○   ○

Read

Explain

Apply

Pray

Morning Reps

○   ○   ○

Big Goal

In ___ days, I will _____

Next Step: _____

Top Tasks	**Est. Time**
○	
○	
○	

If Time

	Est. Time
○	
○	
○	
○	
○	
○	
○	
○	
○	

Evening Prep

○   ○   ○

Read

- -

Explain

- -

Apply

- -

Pray

WEDNESDAY

Morning Reps

○ ○ ○

Big Goal

In ___ days, I will _____

Next Step: _____

Top Tasks

Est. Time

○

○

○

If Time

○

○

○

○

○

○

○

○

○

Evening Prep

○ ○ ○

Read

Explain

Apply

Pray

THURSDAY   / /

Morning Reps

○   ○   ○

- -

Big Goal

In ___ days, I will _____

Next Step: _____

- -

Top Tasks   Est. Time

○

○

○

If Time

○

○

○

○

○

○

○

○

○

- -

Evening Prep

○   ○   ○

Read

Explain

Apply

Pray

/ /

Morning Reps

○   ○   ○

- -

Big Goal

In ___ days, I will _____

Next Step: _____

- -

Top Tasks   Est. Time

○

○

○

If Time

○

○

○

○

○

○

○

○

○

- -

Evening Prep

○   ○   ○

Read

Explain

Apply

Pray

WEEKEND REVIEW

Biggest win

Greatest problem

Possible solutions to the problem:

Relationship Goals

Who	What	When
○		
○		
○		
○		
○		
○		
○		

Goal

In _____ days, I will _____

- -

This Week's Next Step:

Accomplished?

○ Yes ○ No

- -

Next Week's Next Step:

- -

Goal Progress

0	25%	50%	75%	100%

25% =

50% =

75% =

100% = Goal Achieved!

"Can any one of you by worrying add a single hour to your life? ... But seek first his kingdom and his righteousness, and all these things will be given to you as well. Therefore do not worry about tomorrow, for tomorrow will worry about itself. Each day has enough trouble of its own."

Matthew 6:27, 33-34 NIV

Week 8

MONDAY

/ /

Morning Reps

○   ○   ○

Big Goal

In ____ days, I will _____

Next Step: _____

Top Tasks	Est. Time
○	
○	
○	

If Time

	Est. Time
○	
○	
○	
○	
○	
○	
○	
○	
○	

Evening Prep

○   ○   ○

Read

Explain

Apply

Pray

TUESDAY

Morning Reps

○   ○   ○

Big Goal

In ____ days, I will _____

Next Step: _____

Top Tasks	Est. Time
○	
○	
○	

If Time

	Est. Time
○	
○	
○	
○	
○	
○	
○	
○	
○	

Evening Prep

○   ○   ○

Read

Explain

Apply

Pray

/ /

Morning Reps

○   ○   ○

- -

Big Goal

In ___ days, I will _____

Next Step: _____

- -

Top Tasks	**Est. Time**
○	
○	
○	

If Time

○	
○	
○	
○	
○	
○	
○	
○	
○	

- -

Evening Prep

○   ○   ○

Read

Explain

Apply

Pray

THURSDAY

/ /

Morning Reps

○   ○   ○

Big Goal

In ____ days, I will _____

Next Step: _____

Top Tasks	Est. Time
○	
○	
○	

If Time

	Est. Time
○	
○	
○	
○	
○	
○	
○	
○	
○	

Evening Prep

○   ○   ○

Read

Explain

Apply

Pray

FRIDAY

/ /

Morning Reps

○   ○   ○

Big Goal

In ____ days, I will _____

Next Step: _____

Top Tasks

Est. Time

○ _____

○ _____

○ _____

If Time

○ _____

○ _____

○ _____

○ _____

○ _____

○ _____

○ _____

○ _____

○ _____

Evening Prep

○   ○   ○

Read

Explain

Apply

Pray

WEEKEND REVIEW

Biggest win

- -

Greatest problem

- -

Possible solutions to the problem:

- -

Relationship Goals

Who	What	When
○		
○		
○		
○		
○		
○		
○		

Goal

In ____ days, I will _____

- -

This Week's Next Step:

Accomplished?

○ Yes   ○ No

- -

Next Week's Next Step:

- -

Goal Progress

0	25%	50%	75%	100%

25% =

50% =

75% =

100% = Goal Achieved!

"We can make our plans, but the Lord determines our steps."

Proverbs 16:9 NLT

Week 9

MONDAY   / /

Morning Reps

○   ○   ○

- -

Big Goal

In ____ days, I will _____

Next Step: _____

- -

Top Tasks   **Est. Time**

○

○

○

If Time

○

○

○

○

○

○

○

○

- -

Evening Prep

○   ○   ○

Read

Explain

Apply

Pray

/ /

Morning Reps

○   ○   ○

Big Goal

In ___ days, I will _____

Next Step: _____

Top Tasks

Est. Time

○

○

○

If Time

○

○

○

○

○

○

○

○

○

Evening Prep

○   ○   ○

Read

Explain

Apply

Pray

WEDNESDAY

/ /

Morning Reps

○　　　　　　　　　　○　　　　　　　　　　○

Big Goal

In ____ days, I will _____

Next Step: _____

Top Tasks   Est. Time

○

○

○

If Time

○

○

○

○

○

○

○

○

○

Evening Prep

○　　　　　　　　　　○　　　　　　　　　　○

Read

- -

Explain

- -

Apply

- -

Pray

THURSDAY

/ /

Morning Reps

○   ○   ○

- -

Big Goal

In ____ days, I will _____

Next Step: _____

- -

Top Tasks   **Est. Time**

○

○

○

If Time

○

○

○

○

○

○

○

○

○

- -

Evening Prep

○   ○   ○

Read

Explain

Apply

Pray

FRIDAY

/   /

Morning Reps

○   ○   ○

- -

Big Goal

In ___ days, I will _____

Next Step: _____

- -

Top Tasks   Est. Time

○

○

○

If Time

○

○

○

○

○

○

○

○

○

Evening Prep

○   ○   ○

Read

Explain

Apply

Pray

WEEKEND REVIEW

Biggest win

- -

Greatest problem

- -

Possible solutions to the problem:

- -

Relationship Goals

Who	What	When
○		
○		
○		
○		
○		
○		
○		

Goal

In ____ days, I will _____

- -

This Week's Next Step:

Accomplished?

○ Yes   ○ No

- -

Next Week's Next Step:

- -

Goal Progress

0	25%	50%	75%	100%

25% =

50% =

75% =

100% = Goal Achieved!

"Whatever your hand finds to do, do it with all your might"

Ecclesiastes 9:10 NIV

Week 10

MONDAY

Morning Reps

○   ○   ○

- -

Big Goal

In ____ days, I will _____

Next Step: _____

- -

Top Tasks   Est. Time

○

○

○

If Time

○

○

○

○

○

○

○

○

○

- -

Evening Prep

○   ○   ○

Read

Explain

Apply

Pray

TUESDAY

／　／

Morning Reps

○　　　　　　　　　　○　　　　　　　　　　○

- -

Big Goal

In ____ days, I will _____

Next Step: _____

- -

Top Tasks	**Est. Time**
○	
○	
○	

If Time

○	
○	
○	
○	
○	
○	
○	
○	
○	

Evening Prep

○　　　　　　　　　　○　　　　　　　　　　○

Read

Explain

Apply

Pray

WEDNESDAY

Morning Reps

○　　　　　　○　　　　　　○

- -

Big Goal

In ____ days, I will _____

Next Step: _____

- -

Top Tasks　　　　　　　　　　　　　　　　　　　　**Est. Time**

○

○

○

If Time

○

○

○

○

○

○

○

○

○

- -

Evening Prep

○　　　　　　○　　　　　　○

Read

Explain

Apply

Pray

THURSDAY

/ /

Morning Reps

○ ○ ○

Big Goal

In ___ days, I will _____

Next Step: _____

Top Tasks   Est. Time

○

○

○

If Time

○

○

○

○

○

○

○

○

○

Evening Prep

○ ○ ○

Read

- -

Explain

- -

Apply

- -

Pray

Morning Reps

○　　　　　　　　○　　　　　　　　○

Big Goal

In ___ days, I will _____

Next Step: _____

Top Tasks	Est. Time
○	
○	
○	

If Time

○	
○	
○	
○	
○	
○	
○	
○	
○	

Evening Prep

○　　　　　　　　○　　　　　　　　○

Read

Explain

Apply

Pray

WEEKEND REVIEW

Biggest win

- -

Greatest problem

- -

Possible solutions to the problem:

- -

Relationship Goals

Who	What	When
○		
○		
○		
○		
○		
○		
○		

Goal

In ____ days, I will _____

- -

This Week's Next Step:

Accomplished?

○ Yes   ○ No

- -

Next Week's Next Step:

- -

Goal Progress

0	25%	50%	75%	100%

25% =

50% =

75% =

100% = Goal Achieved!

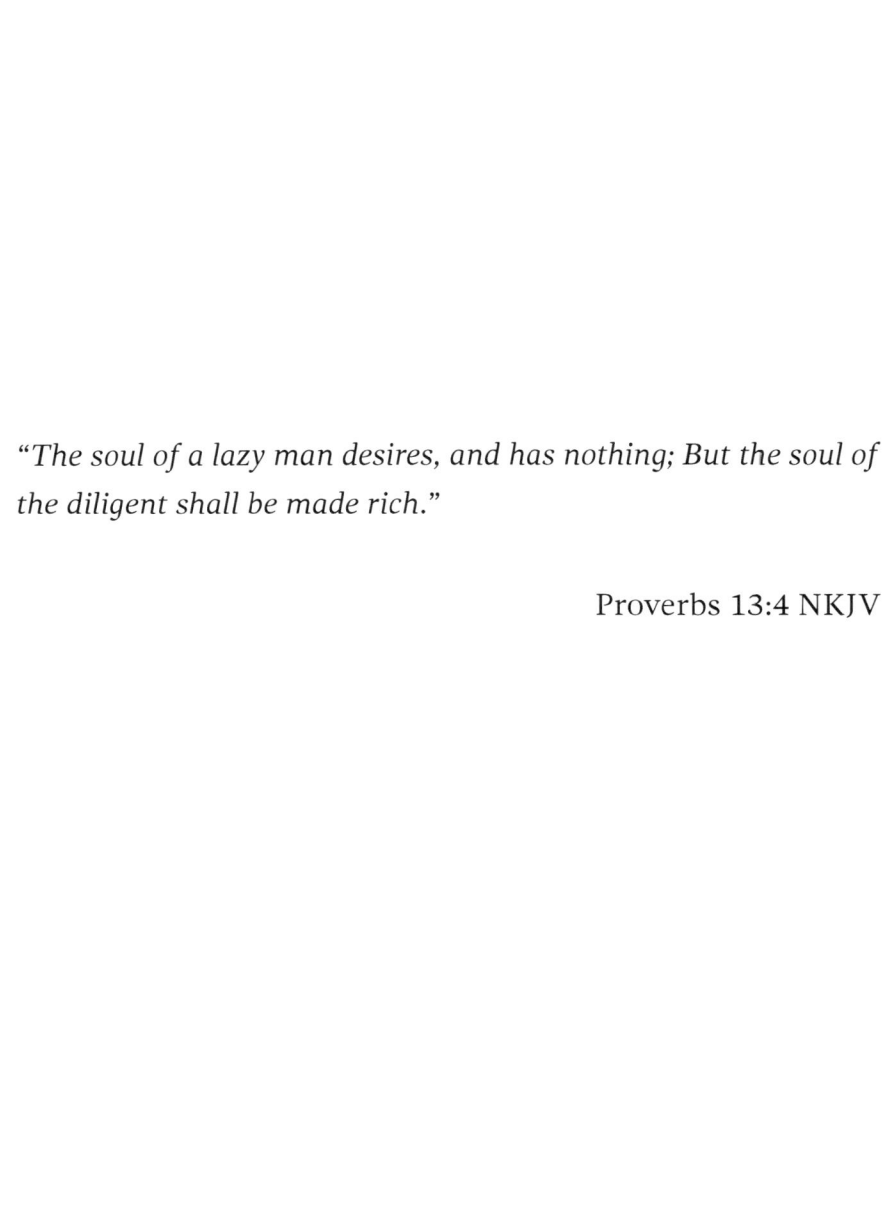

"The soul of a lazy man desires, and has nothing; But the soul of the diligent shall be made rich."

Proverbs 13:4 NKJV

Week 11

MONDAY

Morning Reps

○   ○   ○

Big Goal

In ___ days, I will _____

Next Step: _____

Top Tasks	Est. Time
○	
○	
○	

If Time

	Est. Time
○	
○	
○	
○	
○	
○	
○	
○	
○	

Evening Prep

○   ○   ○

Read

- -

Explain

- -

Apply

- -

Pray

TUESDAY

/ /

Morning Reps

○   ○   ○

Big Goal

In ＿＿＿ days, I will ＿＿＿＿＿＿＿＿＿＿＿＿＿＿＿＿＿

Next Step: ＿＿＿＿＿＿＿＿＿＿＿＿＿＿＿＿＿＿＿＿＿

Top Tasks   Est. Time

○

○

○

If Time

○

○

○

○

○

○

○

○

○

Evening Prep

○   ○   ○

Read

Explain

Apply

Pray

WEDNESDAY

/ /

Morning Reps

○   ○   ○

- -

Big Goal

In ____ days, I will _____

Next Step: _____

- -

Top Tasks   Est. Time

○

○

○

If Time

○

○

○

○

○

○

○

○

○

- -

Evening Prep

○   ○   ○

Read

Explain

Apply

Pray

THURSDAY

Morning Reps

○   ○   ○

- -

Big Goal

In ___ days, I will _____

Next Step: _____

- -

Top Tasks   Est. Time

○

○

○

If Time

○

○

○

○

○

○

○

○

○

- -

Evening Prep

○   ○   ○

Read

Explain

Apply

Pray

FRIDAY

/ /

Morning Reps

○   ○   ○

Big Goal

In ____ days, I will _____

Next Step: _____

Top Tasks

Est. Time

○

○

○

If Time

○

○

○

○

○

○

○

○

○

Evening Prep

○   ○   ○

Read

- -

Explain

- -

Apply

- -

Pray

WEEKEND REVIEW

Biggest win

- -

Greatest problem

- -

Possible solutions to the problem:

- -

Relationship Goals

Who	What	When
○		
○		
○		
○		
○		
○		
○		

Goal

In ___ days, I will _____

- -

This Week's Next Step:

Accomplished?

○ Yes ○ No

- -

Next Week's Next Step:

- -

Goal Progress

0	25%	50%	75%	100%

25% =

50% =

75% =

100% = Goal Achieved!

"So, whether you eat or drink, or whatever you do, do everything for the glory of God."

1 Corinthians 10:31 CSB

Week 12

MONDAY

/ /

Morning Reps

○　　　　　　　　　○　　　　　　　　　○

- -

Big Goal

In ___ days, I will _____

Next Step: _____

- -

Top Tasks   Est. Time

○ |

○ |

○ |

If Time

○ |

○ |

○ |

○ |

○ |

○ |

○ |

○ |

○ |

- -

Evening Prep

○　　　　　　　　　○　　　　　　　　　○

Read

Explain

Apply

Pray

TUESDAY

/ /

Morning Reps

○ ○ ○

- -

Big Goal

In ___ days, I will _____

Next Step: _____

- -

Top Tasks   Est. Time

○

○

○

If Time

○

○

○

○

○

○

○

○

○

- -

Evening Prep

○ ○ ○

168

Read

Explain

Apply

Pray

WEDNESDAY

/ /

Morning Reps

○　　　　　　　　○　　　　　　　　○

Big Goal

In ___ days, I will _____

Next Step: _____

Top Tasks

Est. Time

○

○

○

If Time

○

○

○

○

○

○

○

○

○

Evening Prep

○　　　　　　　　○　　　　　　　　○

Read

Explain

Apply

Pray

Morning Reps

○　　　　　　　　○　　　　　　　　○

Big Goal

In ____ days, I will _____

Next Step: _____

Top Tasks　　　　　　　　　　　　　　　　　　　Est. Time

○

○

○

If Time

○

○

○

○

○

○

○

○

○

Evening Prep

○　　　　　　　　○　　　　　　　　○

Read

Explain

Apply

Pray

FRIDAY

Morning Reps

○　　　　　　　　○　　　　　　　　○

- -

Big Goal

In ___ days, I will _____

Next Step: _____

- -

Top Tasks　　　　　　　　　　　　　　　　　　　　**Est. Time**

○

○

○

If Time

○

○

○

○

○

○

○

○

○

- -

Evening Prep

○　　　　　　　　○　　　　　　　　○

Read

Explain

Apply

Pray

WEEKEND REVIEW

Biggest win

- -

Greatest problem

- -

Possible solutions to the problem:

- -

Relationship Goals

Who	What	When
○		
○		
○		
○		
○		
○		
○		

Goal

In ___ days, I will _____

- -

This Week's Next Step:

Accomplished?

○ Yes ○ No

- -

Next Week's Next Step:

- -

Goal Progress

0	25%	50%	75%	100%

25% =

50% =

75% =

100% = Goal Achieved!

Done

Congratulations! You've completed twelve weeks of productive Christian journaling. Look back and see all the progress you've made. How does it feel?

If you found this process helpful, you can continue it in any journal (you don't have to use my book). But if you'd like to save time writing each section every day, you're welcome to pick up another copy of the Productive Christian Journal and begin your next twelve weeks. Either way, my family and I thank you for supporting our ministry. May God bless you as you continue to make the best use of your time for his glory.

Copyright

Printed in Great Britain
by Amazon